The Markov Chain

Ted Pearson

The Markov Chain

Shearsman Books

First published in the United Kingdom in 2017 by
Shearsman Books
50 Westons Hill Drive
Emersons Green
BRISTOL
BS16 7DF

Shearsman Books Ltd Registered Office
30–31 St. James Place, Mangotsfield, Bristol BS16 9JB
(this address not for correspondence)

www.shearsman.com

ISBN 978-1-84861-533-5

ACKNOWLEDGEMENTS
Some of these poems first appeared in *4ink7*, and
in the anthology, *Resist Much, Obey Little*.

Contents

for Larry Price & Craig Watson

lambeaux maudits d'une phrase absurde

– Stéphane Mallarmé

ONE

1.

Early autumn blueprints

    a new theogony.
        Transcendental wasps build

            nests of pure duration.

Neighborly aporia

    serve topical drinks.
        The streets are abuzz

            with seasonal aperçus.

2.

From deadbeat debutantes,

  songs of ruination,
    gritty murmurations

     that spell the end of days.

In the province of wounds,

  we anticipate scars.
   The years between lovers

    were spent on belay.

3.

We know of your cravings

    for granular data.
        You must trust your

                reptilian brain for relief.

It's clear that you've had

    some synaptic misgivings.
        Would a beautiful corpse

                offer grounds for belief?

4.

A bitter wind assumes

    the shape of a trumpet.
       Utopian silence wants

            a bright patch of noise.

As the sky in the window

    grows dark on the page,
       the Meistersingers enter,

           singing "Tears of Rage."

5.

A terror of typos

    and dismal enclosures
       alike trouble graphemes

           and free-range composers.

Where the punctum encrypts

    the site of transgression,
      the studium backlights

          a tale of repression.

6.

An aging magus

      forages for fragrant dreams.
         He is weary of sorting

            through noxious extremes.

He cohabits with angels –

      they're far from extinct –
         though the city of angels

            is not where you'd think.

7.

A very few centaurs

      survived their narration.
          Now they labor as extras

          in classical texts.

The scent of dead flowers

      pervades the dead garden
      where the Sun God

          in arkestral majesty rests.

8.

We were deaf to the cries

      that urged flight upon us
        and blind to the deaths

           we were callously promised.

But we do know the fate

      of those once put to rout
        in the midst of defending

           this ruined redoubt.

9.

These formal restrictions

    are like benedictions.
        Forgive our presumption,

            but we did go their bail.

Constraints lead to freedoms

    exceeding predictions.
        The tain of the mirror

            is where all poses fail.

10.

By sunset we've itemized

    all our part objects.
        We return to our cells

            when the chapel bell rings.

At one with the dark,

    we embrace our seclusion
        and meditate nightly

            on the thingness of things.

11.

Short days lit by distant sun

      bring us little cheer.
          Now it's time to walk away

               from yet another year.

As the season attests

      with its anthems of doom,
          more than time may be lost

               when a life drops its bloom.

12.

We demand compensation

    for our state-sponsored fears.
      We will take back the lives

        that have slipped through the cracks.

Though the best teachers

    taught us to play things by ear,
      what we hear must be more

        than a symptom of lack.

13.

These wildflowers balk

    at extravagant vases,
        The subtlest of blossoms

            wants sunlight, not glazes.

In our search for a gesture

    as good as its word,
        we discovered a glyph

        that denotes the Absurd.

14.

Of necessity, art must

    exceed its techniques,
        which in turn must endure

        its complaints to the choir

about dead-ends and roadblocks

    and endless critiques
        from irregulars holding

        its feet to the fire.

15.

We share an affinity

> (lest we forget) for
> the words we have fashioned

>> from a mute alphabet.

But while silence may be

> the key to our practice,
> we cleave to those pages

>> whose noises attract us.

16.

Though all ends are certain,

        some arrive much too soon.
                Must we spend our last nights

                        keeping tabs on the moon?

In memory's palace

        of twisted relations,
                true love is a foundry

                        for true abnegation.

17.

You are not who you said

        we would think you to be,
            so we're holding an inquest

            at Chez Misérable.

With your manuscripts bound,

        it's your life on the shelf
            and the syntax you thought

            you could keep to yourself.

18.

You cannot reduce art

     to a timeless kernel
        nor trust to the thought

          that your words are eternal.

After years of dismissals

     and kicks to the curb,
        it is context alone that

          redeems your last words.

19.

How long is the time being?

What counts as being?
Who does the counting

and who's overseeing?

Between riots and romance

we all pay our dues.
But when we need consoling

we play us some blues.

20.

You must trust to the stillness

      of the late night air
          lest the maestra's words fade

          as fast as they flared.

While her thought is

      an engine of textual bliss,
          it's a lock her libretto

          won't end with a kiss.

21.

We're agreed. This will be

    your last incarnation.
        But which one came first?

                Was it chicken or waffles?

Soufflés will collapse

    if they're jostled by karma.
        Our door's always open

             to friends of the dharma.

22.

The proverbial fly

     that interprets the wine
         tells of truths neither simple

         nor true for all time.

On history's jukebox,

     with its stories of throngs,
         the last singer we play

         will be sung by his song.

23.

Her pleasure's the vessel

    that decants her desire
        when she drinks to the outcome

        to which she aspires.

Her portfolio could use

    some winners, they say,
        but her calculus can't mend

        its deviant ways.

24.

Recollections of childhood

    aren't to be trusted.
        We assume you'll plead out

            if you don't pass the buck.

While it's true crimes of passion

    are lacking in thought,
        pure reason's resurgence

           is contingent on luck.

25.

When the audience rose

> with its anger unfurled
>> and instead of applause

>>> hurled abuse at the cast,

it showed that to suffer

> is to be of this world.
>> It takes a dead language

>>> to dwell in the past.

26.

The Marvelous argues

        for variant endings
            and heavily favors

                supernal beginnings.

But absent a telos

        for these meditations,
            their logic is pleased

                to invite divagations.

TWO

27.

Globalized networks

    derealize the locals.
        The proof is compelling,

            although anecdotal.

The agora, at present,

    display's little wit,
        and the stalls offer little

            that you'd call legit.

28.

With their bad sectors scrubbed

    by rhyme and by reason,
        the monads are back.

            They enjoyed the off season.

There can be no grand schema

    without certain gaps,
        some heady inversions,

           and a storied perhaps.

29.

Musical metaphors

     seek reciprocity.
         Breakneck unison

              is mere virtuosity.

Ballads, however, must

     proceed with discretion
         to navigate nuance

              by way of inflection.

30.

We've just about had it

       with speech-acts in speedos.
          Is the beach where their

             soi disant agency leads?

These sand grains want counting

       like potholes want filling.
          It's our understanding that

             slack-time needs killing.

31.

While most true believers

    will not be persuaded,
        catastrophes can't be

        abated by prayer.

If you like, you can outsource

    your congregants' fate.
        Where the future's for sale

        it's the future at stake.

32.

In a duet no more than

    a heartbeat from prose,
        dancers circle each other

            like thorns on a rose.

They seem one with the air

    as they make their last leap.
        But the moment they land,

            their charade is complete.

33.

The days grow longer

      in our lost Eden's thickets
          where exactitude labors

               from dawn's early light.

We're then serenaded

      by amative crickets
          when we bring our exactitude

          in for the night.

34.

While Orpheus ponders

      his lyric redactions,
            his betrothed must retrace

                her own footsteps to hell.

The Lord of the Underworld's

      tired of abstractions.
            When she reaches his throne

                he says, *Babe, you look swell.*

35.

Repetition with a difference

       makes a difference.
           She brokers relations

                with her yen still intact.

Where gall can be rendered

       as impish presumption,
           her lovers' embraces are

                fraught with assumptions.

36.

When the pink slips arrived,

    we went off the deep end.
        Our bar tabs depend

           on a regular stipend.

Where the bosses want only

    to turn back the clock,
        their desire is regressive.

           Their rationale, shlock.

37.

Overanxious actuaries

    time-stamp our doom
      while the gatekeeper sings

        of his favorite things:

nefarious memoirs –

    erotic translations –
      ideas of order –

        knishes … durations.

38.

Your body reproaches

      the role that would play you
          and the well-crafted gown

             that amply displays you

as the weary chanteuse

      who essays "Love for Sale."
          The gist of the lyric

             tells a whole other tale.

39.

When your pipe dreams defer

        to your curious joy
            at the prospect of leaving

                your bed for the day,

you pack up your axe,

        which is light as a toy,
            and then head to the woodshed.

            You're ready to play.

40.

A store-bought bouquet

> makes a studied impression
> with bevies of blossoms

>> that were forced till they peaked.

When the People say *we,*

> they don't mean you and me.
> The consensus they're seeking

>> will set no one free.

41.

The script was finessed

    with wit and agility.
        Its endgame bears witness

        to its nobility.

At long last the sun's gotten

    over that rainbow,
        who now works the circuit

        as part of a sideshow.

42.

Immortality escaped us

      exactly when?
           A series of quilting points

           sutures our years.

The good may die young,

      but we're better than ever.
           I'll take even odds

           we see sunrise together.

43.

Brocaded cadenzas

    bewilder the keyboard.
      The silence that follows

          puts the players on edge.

Which thread must they pull

    to regain their composure –
      slow semiquavers

          or a time-lapse exposure?

44.

Recollections of ecstasy …

      toujours … c'est tout …
          may inspire songs of love,

               but no longer for you.

The guides chat up tourists

      and then take them to school
          to get shots of the spots

               where I once played the fool.

45.

Stories teach by telling.

  Narrative wants your child.
      At their best they allay

          youthful fears and complaints.

The question is where

      can we trade in the plot line
          for a manifold text

              and the world it creates?

46

The dune grasses sway

      as the desert wind glosses
         a topography desolate

         as it is vast.

A begging bowl filled

      with unspeakable loss
         is the only reminder

         of sojourners past.

47.

After deep cuts in lean years

        resulted in scars,
                we fixed up the spare room,

                then we went to the bar.

When drowning your sorrows,

        just swim for the bottom
           and wait for the quartet

                to play "Early Autumn."

48.

A deathbed reprieve

    is a teachable moment.
       Your range of emotions

          is one with its quotient.

Where the least bit of sunlight

    appears as a sign,
       a daydream's a nomad

          in the arcades of time.

49.

Aggregations of integers,

    largely unsung,
        duly translate personae

            who parley in tongues.

Where the lyrics of loss

    are most bitter indeed,
        between spirit and letter

            there's nothing to read.

50.

We studied scale models

    of the dangers we face
      from the bigoted grifter

        whose bile grows apace.

Whose mind-boggling edicts

    we hear on the hour.
      Whose untrammeled ego

        is dumb as a flower.

51.

Would more precise surveys

    establish a homeland
      for scintillant ciphers

        as bearers of meaning?

Both the crystal and flame

    are forms of perfection
      that foster reflection

        without intervening.

52.

We are doomed to recall

    what we'd rather forget.
      The system of systems

        is the set of all sets.

The tracks of our tears

    lead to immiseration.
      It's time to change trains

        or at least destinations.

www.ingramcontent.com/pod-product-compliance
Lightning Source LLC
Chambersburg PA
CBHW031935080426
42734CB00007B/691